For the Father Whom God Created:

_____

B
B
Brighton Books
Nashville, TN

Fathers

Fathers

by Jim Gallery

Table of Contents

BRIGHTON BOOKS
Nashville, TN 37204

ISBN 1-58334-113-7

The quoted ideas expressed in this book (but not scripture verses) are not, in all cases, exact quotations, as some have been edited for clarity and brevity. In all cases, the author has attempted to maintain the speaker's original intent. In some cases, quoted material for this book was obtained from secondary sources, primarily print media. While every effort was made to ensure the accuracy of these sources, the accuracy cannot be guaranteed. For additions, deletions, corrections or clarifications in future editions of this text, please write BRIGHTON BOOKS.

Printed in the United States of America
Cover Design & Page Layout: *Bart Dawson*

1 2 3 4 5 6 7 8 9 10 • 01 02 03 04 05 06 07 08 09 10

Acknowledgments: The author is indebted to Criswell Freeman for his support and friendship and to the helpful staff at Walnut Grove Press.

To Steve Trinkle
A Godly Man, Husband, and Father

Introduction

All things great and small are created by God—including fathers. God intends that fathers protect their families, love their families, and provide for their families. God intends that fathers teach Biblical truths by word and by example. God creates fathers in order that they might fulfill their responsibilities as they follow His Word.

The purpose of this book, through scripture, stories, quotes, and sayings, is to encourage God-fearing fathers in the awesome responsibility of raising their children and loving their families. Our children, of course, are on loan from God, and they deserve our very best. God blesses the father who blesses His children.

Daily life is like the underside of a hand-stitched rug. As human beings, we see only the bottom side of the rug; although the rug may contain many colorful threads, its patterns are often confusing, and its designs are often unclear. God, however, sees the finished product, the topside of the rug. God sees a beautiful design with every thread in place. When we study God's word and follow His commandments, we glimpse—albeit incompletely—the beautiful pattern that God intends for His children…and for our own.

Chapter 1

and God Created Fathers...
Who Love

————◆————

Be imitators of God, therefore, as dearly loved
children and live a life of love, just as Christ
loved us and gave himself up for us as a
fragrant offering and sacrifice to God.

Ephesians 5:1,2

A young boy was scheduled to play in his first basketball game. The boy's father knew little of the sport but attended the game with the clear purpose of cheering on his boy. After the tip-off, the ball was knocked loose, and a mad scramble ensued. The father watched his son recover the ball, dribble to the basket, and score. Unfortunately, in the confusion of the moment, the boy had turned himself around, dribbled to the wrong goal, and scored points for the other team. Oblivious to his son's mistake, the proud father jumped up and screamed, "That's my boy! That's my boy!"

The father was uninformed in the rules of basketball but wise in the ways of parenting. Loving parents support their children through triumphs and trials, through good times and bad. Wise parents separate the behaviors of their children from the children themselves. Wise fathers know that a child's behavior can be applauded or corrected, but that a father's love for his child, like God's love for His children, is to be unconditional.

To be loved and to know love is a basic human need. Thoughtful fathers recognize this need and behave accordingly. Sometimes, in the rush of daily living, even the most well-intentioned dads may become so concerned with providing material provisions for their families that they leave precious little time for the emotional and spiritual leadership that God intends. Of course, love cannot be bought with material possessions; yet, fathers may find themselves working harder and longer to buy things for their children, when what their children really need is more time with dad.

God created fathers to love their children without reservation or condition. Even when a boy or girl makes an embarrassing mistake, even when he or she scores points for the other team, God never withholds His love, and neither should we. So what do you say fathers? How about a great big cheer for your children? Altogether now: "Gimme an "L"....Gimme "O"....

If I speak with human eloquence and angelic ecstasy but don't
love, I'm nothing but the creaking of a rusty gate.
If I speak God's Word with power, revealing all his mysteries and
making everything plain as day, and if I have faith
that says to a mountain, "Jump," and it jumps,
but I don't have love, I'm nothing.
If I give everything I own to the poor and even go to the stake to
be burned as a martyr, but I don't love,
I've gotten nowhere.
So, no matter what I say, what I believe, and what I do,
I'm bankrupt without love.

1 Corinthians 13:1-3 The Message

God is love; and he that dwelleth in love dwelleth
in God, and God in him.

1 John 4:16 KJV

Love is....a steady wish for the loved person's
ultimate good....

C. S. Lewis

He who is filled with love is filled with God Himself.

St. Augustine

He that loveth not, knoweth not God;
for God is love.

1 John 4:8 KJV

As the Father hath loved me, so have I loved you:
continue ye in my love. If ye keep my
commandments, ye shall abide in my love;
even as I have kept my Father's commandments,
and abide in his love.

John 15:9-10 KJV

Inasmuch as love grows in you, so beauty grows.
For love is the beauty of the soul.

St. Augustine

And, ye fathers, provoke not your children to wrath:
bring them up in the nurture and
admonition of the Lord.

Ephesians 6:4 KJV

Kids go where there is excitement.
They stay where there is love.

Zig Ziglar

Give me such love for God and men as will
blot out all hatred and bitterness.

Dietrich Bonhoeffer

Children's children are the crown of old men;
and the glory of children are their fathers.

Proverbs 17:6 KJV

and God Created Fathers...
Who Care

———◆◆———

So, chosen by God for this new life of love, dress in
the wardrobe God picked out for you: compassion,
kindness, humility, quiet strength, discipline.
Be even-tempered, content with second place,
quick to forgive an offense. Forgive as quickly and
completely as the Master forgave you. And regardless
of what else you put on, wear love. It's your basic,
all-purpose garment. Never be without it.

Colossians 3:12-14 The Message

The Gospels paint a picture of a compassionate Jesus helping people everywhere He went. Matthew writes, "Jesus went through all the towns and villages, teaching in their synagogues, preaching the good news of the kingdom and healing every disease and sickness. When he saw the crowds, he had compassion on them...." (Matthew 9:35,36)

Godly fathers exhibit the same kind of compassion for others that Jesus showed to his followers. When fathers follow Christ's example, they, in turn, become powerful examples to their children. If children are to understand God the Father, they need to see God in their fathers. Amid the demands of daily living, it is easy for well-intentioned men to overlook the needs of their neighbors. But the busier life becomes, the more we need to slow down and listen to God.

When we take time each day to talk to God in prayer, He redirects our thoughts and actions. When we take time to reflect on God's word, He leads us in the paths of righteousness. When we slow down long enough to listen to the Giver of All Things Good, He speaks a clear and simple message: "A new commandment I give unto you, That ye love one another; as I have loved you...." (John 13:34 KJV)

The life of Jesus is a model for compassionate living. Fathers take note. The compassionate life is the godly life. It is God's way and His commandment, now and forever.

＊＊＊

Do all the good you can.
By all the means you can.
In all the ways you can.
In all the places you can.
At all the times you can.
To all the people you can.
As long as ever you can.

John Wesley

Jesus had an unselfish heart. If he lives in us,
selfishness will not predominate.

Billy Graham

We are never more like God than when we give.

Chuck Swindoll

If you want your neighbor to know what Christ
will do for him, let the neighbor see what
Christ has done for you.

Henry Ward Beecher

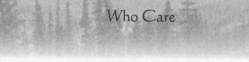

It is the duty of every Christian
to be Christ to his neighbor.

Martin Luther

In everything, therefore, treat people the same way
you want them to treat you, for this is the Law
and the Prophets.

Matthew 7:12 NASB

Be kindly affectioned one to another with
brotherly love; in honor preferring one another;
not slothful in business; fervent in spirit;
serving the Lord; rejoicing in hope;
patient in tribulation;
continuing instant in prayer....

Romans 12:10-12 KJV

Honor all men. Love the brotherhood.
Fear God. Honor the king.

1 Peter 2:17 KJV

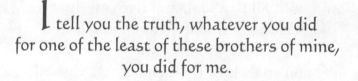

I tell you the truth, whatever you did
for one of the least of these brothers of mine,
you did for me.

Matthew 25:40 NIV

Jesus said unto him, Thou shalt love
the Lord thy God with all thy heart,
and with all thy soul, and with all thy mind.
This is the first and great commandment.
And the second is like unto it,
Thou shalt love thy neighbor as thyself.
On these two commandments hang
all the law and the prophets.

Matthew 22:37-40 KJV

Chapter 3

and God Created Fathers...
Who Encourage

And let us consider how we may spur one another
on toward love and good deeds. Let us not give up
meeting together, as some are in the habit of doing,
but let us encourage one another – and all the more
as you see the Day approaching.

Hebrews 10:24,25

The first two years of my life were spent at the University of Florida where my father attended journalism school. He received his degree, and, after a brief foray into the wholesale grocery business, began a lifelong newspaper career.

My dad was a great encourager to my sisters and me. Despite physical ailments, many related to war injuries, my father lived life with happiness and humor. He encouraged my family and all who knew him with his resilience and optimism. He not only coped with the difficulties of life, he overcame them.

Communication was Dad's strong suit, and he expressed himself best on paper. Many times, when the subject was important, Dad would write a note or letter expressing his feelings and giving his thoughts. Sometimes, he would simply hand me the missive without comment; sometimes, he added a word or two of explanation. But, whatever the topic, Dad always included words of encouragement and words of blessing, and I was always the better for it.

In college I majored in Political Science and soon found myself working for a United States Congressman. Not surprisingly, I planned on becoming a lawyer and entering politics. But God had a different idea: the ministry. When the Lord called me into full-time Christian service, my father wrote words of support and approval that expressed his pride in me. Today, a full quarter of a century after those words were penned, they still comfort me.

Through actions, writings, and words, my father made it absolutely clear that I was a blessing and a delight to him. Today, many years after his death, I still treasure his approval. Without reservation, I can say my father's life was blessed because of me. An arrogant statement? No! My father told me so.

Because of Dad's encouragement, I live with a sense of belonging. Wherever my life's journey takes me, I have a place I belong: my family. My father gave me that gift. His encouragement gave me an enduring sense of self-worth. Whatever hand is dealt me in this capricious world, I am okay. If others belittle me and circumstances indicate I have failed, I know I am not a failure. My father gave me that gift.

We all seek security, and we seek it through many avenues: money, power, education, popularity, to name but a few. Yet, these forms of security are never failsafe; indeed, they are always temporary. Ultimate security *does* exist, but it is not found in material possessions or in the approval of man. Ultimate security is, first and foremost, the protection we find in God, and, second, the security we find in family. Lucky children live their days knowing that whatever may happen, they are secure in their Father's love as well as their fathers' love.

The scripture urges us to be inventive and creative in inspiring love and in helping others. God intends that fathers offer a sense of belonging, security, and self-worth to their children. These offering are best packaged in unconditional love. Godly fathers should ask themselves, "What gift of encouragement can I give my children today?" After all, our children are God's gift to us as we are God's gift to them.

My father no longer walks this earth, but his encouragement will be with me forever. I also want my children to receive that same type of encouragement from me. After all, our heavenly Father has given His children encouragement, and we, as His followers, should do no less for our own.

...encourage one another daily....

Hebrews 3:13

The apostle Paul writes that your words ought to be a gift to others:

Do not let any unwholesome talk come out of your mouths, but only what is helpful for building others up according to their needs, that it may benefit those who listen.

Ephesians 4:29

The father who carefully measures the words that come from his mouth can give the gift of encouragement continuously.

Encouragement

To give courage and hope;
To cheer;
To motivate;
To inspire;
To hearten;
To invigorate;
To give confidence;
To give boldness.

God of our life, there are days when the burdens
we carry chafe our shoulders and weigh us down;
when the road seems dreary and endless
the skies grey and threatening; when our lives
have no music in them, and our hearts are lonely,
and our souls have lost their courage.
Flood the path with light, run our eyes to where
the skies are full of promise; tune our hearts to brave
music; give us the sense of comradeship with heroes
and saints of every age; and so quicken our spirits
that we may be able to encourage the souls of
all who journey with us on the road of life,
to Your honour and glory.

St. Augustine

Encouragement is the oxygen of the soul.

John Maxwell

God grant that we may not hinder those who
are battling their way slowly into the light.

Oswald Chambers

How many people stop because so few say, "Go!"

Chuck Swindoll

He climbs highest who helps another up.

Zig Ziglar

39

Joseph, a Levite from Cyprus, whom the
apostles called Barnabas (which means
Son of Encouragement), sold a field
he owned and brought the money and
put it at the apostles' feet.

Acts 4:36,37 NIV

———◆———

How will you be remembered?
Will you be remembered as an encouraging
husband and father?
May you be a daily beacon of encouragement
to your family.

Chapter 4

and God Created Fathers...
Who Celebrate Life

This is the day the Lord has made;
let us rejoice and be glad in it.

Psalm 118:24

I first met Ross White when he visited my church. His firm handshake, ready smile, and gregarious nature strongly suggested to me that I wanted to make Ross a friend. I have always tried to surround myself with positive people who enjoy life, and Ross certainly seemed to fit that description. But little did I know that to Ross White, life is not simply a positive experience, it is a continuous celebration. Whether he is practicing law, or playing drums in his band, or teaching Sunday School, or enjoying his family, Ross is having fun—and lots of it. Ross celebrates life, and his joy is contagious.

Ross White teaches his senior adult Sunday School class with the kind of gusto and enthusiasm that would make an old-time revivalist look tame. When Ross organizes a class party (which is quite often), even the youth of the church take notice of the fun. Ross and his class members seem to have taken Paul's admonition to the Thessalonian church seriously: "Be joyful always...give thanks in all circumstances, for this is God's will for you in Christ Jesus." (1 Thessalonians 5:16,18)

Too many Christians seem to forget that every day with Jesus is meant to be celebrated, not tolerated. Too many Christians forget that God is great and God is good all day long, not just at the dinner table. Too many Christians seem slow to make a joyful noise, or, for that matter, even a joyful peep. But not Ross White. Ross is a living, breathing example of joyous Christian living, and we all would do well to imitate his enthusiasm.

Bill Hybels, senior pastor at Willow Creek Community Church, said that all people need to celebrate others and to be celebrated themselves. He was right. And it is worth remembering that celebration is a choice, a decision to count one's blessings and to act accordingly. The choice to celebrate is the choice to live a full and happy life. John Maxwell, in his book *The Winning Attitude*, writes, "Do you feel the world is treating you well? If your attitude toward the world is excellent, you will receive excellent results. If you feel so-so about the world, your response from that world will be average. Feel badly about your world, and you will seem to have only negative feedback from life."

Children need fathers who celebrate life. Young people will learn soon enough that life isn't always fair as they endure the inevitable hardships and sorrows that accompany life here on earth. In a difficult world, children need fathers who clearly demonstrate the power of joyous Christianity.

So dads, be creative: Find new ways to celebrate this wonderful life that God has given you and yours. And if you find yourself fresh out of creative ideas for celebrating God's gifts, you can always ask Ross White. He is easy to find: Ross is either at home, at work, or at church...celebrating!

Claim the joy that is yours. Pray. And know
that your joy is used by God to reach others.

Kay Arthur

Rejoicing is clearly a spiritual command.
To ignore it, I need to remind you,
is disobedience.

Charles Swindoll

I approach prayer in a similar way as I experience
the joy of relationship with God. No matter
how severe "the winter of the soul" may have been,
standing in the presence of God brings pure joy.

Henry Blackaby

The true joy of a man's life is in his
relationship to God.

Oswald Chambers

There is not one blade of grass,
there is no color in this world that is not
intended to make us rejoice.

John Calvin

...let the hearts of those who seek the Lord rejoice.
Look to the Lord and his strength;
seek his face always.

1 Chronicles 16: 10-11 NIV

These things have I spoken unto you,
that my joy might remain in you,
and that your joy might be full.

John 15:11 KJV

I will thank you, Lord with all my heart;
I will tell of all the marvelous things you have done.
I will be filled with joy because of you.
I will sing praises to your name, O Most High.

Psalm 9:1-2 NLT

Rejoice evermore. Pray without ceasing.
In every thing give thanks: for this is the will
of God in Christ Jesus concerning you.

1 Thessalonians 5:16-18 KJV

Verily, verily, I say unto you,
Whatsoever ye shall ask the Father
in my name, he will give it you.
Hitherto have ye asked nothing
in my name: ask, and ye shall receive,
that your joy may be full.

John 16:23-24 KJV

The ability to rejoice in any situation
is a sign of spiritual maturity.

Billy Graham

Chapter 5

and God Created Fathers...
Who Live Faithfully and
Rightly Before God

...but the righteous will live by his faith....
Habakkuk 2:4

We can all identify with the prophet Habakkuk who, in anguish, cries out to the Lord. Habakkuk's world is topsy-turvy. Goodness appears defeated while evil flourishes. Habakkuk wonders aloud if God is listening to his cries. And the prophet ponders why God doesn't do something. Now.

God responds that godly men must be patient and put their trust in the Lord of justice. God declares that life is an exercise in righteous living and faithfulness, no matter our circumstances.

God created us in order that we might commit ourselves to Him and His way. When we do, an amazing thing happens:

Though the fig tree does not bud
and there are no grapes on the vines,
though the olive crop fails
and the fields produce no food,
though there are no sheep in the pen
and no cattle in the stalls,
yet I will rejoice in the LORD,
I will be joyful in God my Savior.
The Sovereign LORD is my strength;
he makes my feet like the feet of a deer,
he enables me to go on the heights.

Habakkuk 3:17-19

God teaches us that the focus of life is to live rightly and faithfully. When we do, the difficulties of the day have little impact on the joy of life. With God's help, the righteous man will "go to the heights" because his faith in God gives him the strength to do so.

Jesus urges us to "...seek first his kingdom and his righteousness, and all these things will be given to you as well." *(Matthew 6:33)* Faithfulness to God results in freedom from worry. Faithfulness to God means viewing difficult circumstances not as some sort of celestial punishment but instead as a conduit for God's grace.

Fathers have much to teach their children about faith. Godly fathers must teach their children to "Love the Lord your God will all your heart and with all your soul and with all your mind." *(Matthew 22:37)* Fathers who model righteousness and teach faithfulness enable their children to do the same.

The Apostle John writes, "...everyone born of God overcomes the world. This is the victory that has overcome the world, even our faith. Who is it that overcomes the world? Only he who believes that Jesus in the Son of God." *(1 John 5:4,5)* God makes an astounding promise: We can overcome the world because Jesus did. Fathers who understand and accept this promise—and share it—leave a priceless gift for future generations.

We must face today as children of tomorrow.
We must meet the uncertainties of this world with
the certainty of the world to come. To the pure in
heart, nothing really bad can happen...
Thus not death but sin should be our great fear.

A. W. Tozer

Let your faith in Christ be in the quiet confidence
that He will every day and every moment keep you
as the apple of His eye, keep you in perfect peace
and in the sure experience of all the light and
the strength you need.

Andrew Murray

Our faith grows by expression. If we want to
keep our faith, we must share it.

Billy Graham

Then he touched their eyes and said,
"According to your faith it will be
done to you"....

Matthew 9:29 NIV

In thee, O Lord, do I put my trust;
let me never be put into confusion.

Psalm 71:1 KJV

Cast your burden upon the Lord and
He will sustain you: He will never allow
the righteous to be shaken.

Psalm 55:22 NASB

I tell you the truth, if you have faith
and do not doubt...
you can say to this mountain
"Go and throw yourself into the sea,"
and it will be done.

Matthew 21:21 NIV

Blessed is the man whose strength
is in thee....

Psalm 84:5 KJV

Faith in God will not get for you everything
you want, but it will get for you what God wants
you to have. The unbeliever does not need
what he wants; the Christian should want
only what he needs.

Vance Havner

The secret of Christian quietness is not indifference,
but the knowledge that God is my Father,
He loves me, and I shall never think of anything
He will forget; then worry becomes an impossibility.

Oswald Chambers

That we may not complain of what is,
let us see God's hand in all events;
and, that we may not be afraid of what shall be,
let us see all events in God's hand.

Matthew Henry

A wise man will hear, and will increase learning; and a man of understanding shall attain unto wise counsels.

Proverbs 1:5 KJV

Faith in God is a terrific venture in the dark.

Oswald Chambers

Chapter 6

and God Created Fathers...
Who Serve Others

...so he got up from the meal, took off his outer clothing,
and wrapped a towel around his waist. After that, he poured
water into a basin and began to wash his disciples' feet,
drying them with the towel that was wrapped around him.

John 13:4,5

Jesus not only preached a message of servant-hood, He modeled it. The same night of His betrayal and arrest, Jesus gathered with his disciples to share a meal. *(John 13)* He used that occasion to teach an important lesson to all of us who call ourselves Christians.

As the disciples reclined around the table, Jesus took a towel, a basin of water, and began to wash their feet. The washing of feet was a task normally reserved for the lowest of servants. Yet, Jesus, the Savior of the world, was washing feet. The whole scene was so preposterous to Simon Peter that he protested to his Master, but Jesus insisted, explaining that if He, as "Teacher" and "Lord," washed their feet, so should the disciples wash each others' feet: "I have set you an example that you should do as I have done for you. I tell you the truth, no servant is greater than his master, nor is a messenger greater than the one who sent him. Now that you know these things, you will be blessed if you do them." *(John 13:15-17)*

A seminary professor once suggested to me that the symbol of Christianity should be a cross with a towel draped over it. His point was this: We Christians should remember the towel as well as the cross. Jesus taught that a servant's spirit is the right attitude for His followers. The apostle Paul writes that we should imitate

Jesus who took on the "very nature of a servant."
(Philippians 2:5-7)

God created fathers to teach and model servanthood to their children. The world teaches "me first" but Jesus teaches "others before me." As a young child, I was taught that joy was a result of:

> <u>J</u>esus first
> <u>O</u>thers second
> <u>Y</u>ourself last

Jesus teaches us that the very act of serving others is a blessing not only for the served but also for the server. If we are to imitate Jesus, we will *reach*—albeit figuratively—for a towel and *teach* our children the joys of serving others. As Christians, we can do no less.

———◆———

There are some things that only God can do, and for us to attempt to do them is to waste our efforts; and there are other things that only man can do, and for us to ask God to do them is to waste our prayers.

A. W. Tozer

Without God, we cannot.
Without us, God will not.

St. Augustine

Have thy tools ready; God will find thee work.

Charles Kingsley

The greatest among you will be your servant. For whoever exalts himself will be humbled, and whoever humbles himself will be exalted.

Matthew 23:11 NIV

Therefore, since we receive a kingdom which
cannot be shaken, let us show gratitude by which
we may offer to God an acceptable service with
reverence and awe....

Hebrews 12:28 NASB

And he sat down, and called the twelve,
and saith unto them, If any man desire to be first
the same shall be last of all, and servant of all.

Mark 9:35 KJV

Freely you have received, freely give.

Matthew 10:8 NIV

He that hath two coats, let him impart to him that
hath none; and he that hath meat,
let him do likewise.

Luke 3:11 KJV

Do not withhold good from those who deserve it
when it is within your power to act.

Proverbs 3:27 NIV

Be careful not to do your acts of righteousness
before men, to be seen by them.
If you do, you will have no reward
from your father in heaven.

Matthew 6:1 NIV

*W*e do the works, but God works
in us in the doing of the works.

St. Augustine

Chapter 7

and God Created Fathers...
Who Patiently Nurture

...but while he [prodigal son] was still a long way off,
his father saw him and was filled with compassion for him;
he ran to his son, threw his arms around him and kissed him.

Luke 15:20

Most 16-year-old children think
their parents know little or nothing.
A few years later, these same children are
amazed at how much their parents have
learned in that short time span.

I've read many variations of the quotation on the previous page, but the message is always the same: Teenagers think they know more than their parents. Almost universally, young people want to venture out on their own by trying out new ideas and behaviors (many times, these ideas are contrary to their parent's sound advice). Eventually, rebellious teenagers discover that their parents were neither naïve nor foolish. To the contrary, parents usually *do* know best.

Luke, in the 15th chapter, records three parables that Jesus shares about the joy that takes place when the lost is found. One of those parables tells the story of a rather amazing father.

This father had two sons: one who stayed home and tended the family business, and another who chose a different path. The rebellious son demanded his inheritance and left. How difficult it must have been for this godly father to allow his son to choose a lifestyle that would lead to his son's despair and distress. After years of teaching his son the values and principles that would lead to a successful life, the father must now allow his son the opportunity to fail.

How often and how long did this loving father stand

at the front door of his home looking out on the horizon, hoping against hope that his son would soon step into sight? The Bible does not tell us the answer to that question, but we do know from experience when any child is in jeopardy, a parent's minutes seem like hours and hours like days.

The father waited and hoped and prayed that his son would return home to a father and family that loved him so. Then one day it happened. The son returned, full of remorse, asking forgiveness, and admitting defeat. His father responded not with "I told you so" but with love and celebration. How joyous was the occasion until the son who *had not* left home saw the celebration and became angry. The elder son felt underappreciated, and he complained to his father. This father would have been totally justified in expressing exasperation to his eldest son, but no. This godly man patiently responded, "My son,...you are always with me and all I have is yours." *(Luke 15:31)* All dads should be so understanding!

The apostle Paul strongly admonishes, "Fathers, do not exasperate your children; instead, bring them up in the training and instruction of the Lord." *(Ephesians 6:4)* Paul also challenges, "Let us not become weary in doing good, for at the proper time we will reap a harvest if we do not give up." *(Galations 6:9)* A father's primary responsibility is not to earn mountains of money nor is it to provide the life of luxury for his family. First and foremost a father is… a father. He instructs his children in the way of the Lord and prepares them to become successful Christian adults. This sort of preparation for life is not easy for any parent; it requires time and patience. But wise fathers know it's worth the effort. And so does God.

If God is diligent, surely we ought to be diligent
in doing our duty to Him. Think how patient and
diligent God has been to us!

Oswald Chambers

Hatred stirs up dissention,
but love covers over all wrongs.

Proverbs 10:12 NIV

Patience is the companion of wisdom.

St. Augustine

For ye have need of patience, that,
after ye have done the will of God,
ye might receive the promise.

Hebrews 10:36 KJV

We urge you, brethren,
admonish the unruly,
encourage the fainthearted,
help the weak,
be patient with everyone.

1 Thessalonians 5:14 NASB

and God Created Fathers...
Who Spend Time with
Their Children

———◆———

Hear, O Israel: The Lord our God, the Lord is one. Love the Lord
your God with all your heart and with all your soul and with
all your strength. These commandments that I give you today
are to be upon your hearts. Impress them on your children.
Talk with them when you sit at home and when you walk along
the road, when you lie down and when you get up. Tie them as
symbols on your hands and bind them on your foreheads.
Write them on the doorframes of your house and on your gates.

Deuteronomy 6:4-9

My work has always allowed me time with my children, and I thank God for that. I didn't miss many field trips when my Julie and Jimmy were in school. I've marched single file through the state capitol with 200 fourth graders (who, by the way, were more excited about the next stop at McDonalds than by the hallowed chambers of state government). I've huddled with students next to the chimpanzee cage when an unexpected, cold fall rainstorm doused the zoo. I've enjoyed wading through the mud (and other surprises) as my child's class learned firsthand about dairy farming.

When I wasn't going on field trips, I was a homeroom father. When class parties were planned, I was present and accounted for, serving Koolaide, cookies, and confections. When my son's elementary school decided that five-year olds in kindergarten needed an hour each week in the computer lab, I was there to assist these young computer wizards. I was humbled to see how five-year-olds grasped the computer age better than I. When my son would draw designs in the dirt between second and third base rather than field ground balls, I was there exhorting, advising, and reminding myself to behave. I even joined four other parents with vans in a carpool during my son's first year in school. It wasn't always easy juggling my schedule to participate in all these school events with my children, but it was always worth it...for them and for me.

There is an argument that "quality time" is more important than "quantity time." In reality, our children need both. First and foremost, children need *quality moments* with parents in church, at home, and at play. But children also need great *quantities* of time with their parents.

God teaches us to instruct our children of His truths. Children learn best when they hear and see lessons many times and in many places. God created fathers to spend time with their children. Lots of time. Nothing is more important. Nothing is more satisfying.

Apart from religious influence, the family
is the most important unit of society.

Billy Graham

Raising children is not unlike
a long-distance race in which
the contestants must learn to
pace themselves. . . .
That is the secret of winning.

James Dobson

Let love and faithfulness never leave you …
write them on the tablet of your heart.

Proverbs 3:3 NIV

No other structure can replace the family.
Without it, our children have no moral foundation.
Without it, they become moral illiterates
whose only law is self.

Chuck Colson

No man hath seen God at any time.
If we love one another, God dwelleth in us ….

1 John 4:12 KJV

Train up a child in the way he should go:
and when he is old, he will not depart from it.

Proverbs 22:6 KJV

A new commandment I give unto you,
That ye love one another; as I have loved you....

John 13:34 KJV

Chapter 9

and God Created Fathers...
Who Discipline in Love

The people I love, I call to account—prod and correct
and guide so that they'll live at their best.
Revelation 3:19 The Message

Floyd Price is fun to be around. Always the storyteller, the teaser, the upbeat, Floyd is the type of man who leaves you feeling a little better about yourself and your world. Floyd's children, now grown, agree their dad is the life of the party, but they also know another facet of his personality: he disciplines those he loves.

Janelle, Erin, and Jimmy grew up in a loving, fun-filled family. Floyd, along with his wife, Bobbie Nell, created a Christian atmosphere where their children could learn about the Lord and His ways. Floyd and Bobbie disciplined their children because they loved their children. It is written, the "Lord disciplines those he loves...." *(Hebrews 12:6)* So do godly parents.

Floyd's philosophy of parent/child relationships was simple: parents should make the rules and children should obey them. Period. When one of the children asked to be allowed to attend a certain event, the conditions were set forth: who was driving, with whom, where, and when. No deviation from that plan could occur without first calling home and receiving approval. Any changes without dad's or mom's OK resulted in unhappy consequences.

All movies in the Price household were first screened

(by one or both parents) before the children were allowed to watch. At Erin's 13th birthday party, a video slipped past the screening process. Along with Erin and 12 other teenage girls, Floyd watched as the movie began. Two minutes into the video, Floyd was troubled. Three minutes later, Floyd told Erin to turn the movie off. Erin was mortified and fled to her room in tears. Floyd followed her, trying to comfort, but standing firm on the principle that certain types of movies would not be allowed in their house.

When Floyd returned to the den, 12 girls were staring at him in total silence. The ever-resourceful Floyd pulled out a deck of cards and commenced with card tricks. Soon the girls were laughing and talking, soon Erin returned the party, and soon everyone, including Erin, was happy again. Floyd had maintained the values of the family, creatively dealt with an awkward situation, and he had taught Erin, in love, that rules would be followed.

A few years later, while Erin was attending college, she listened to many of her friends tell horror stories about the lack of discipline in their lives. She wrote her father thanking him for loving her enough to care, to discipline, and to be consistent.

John records the words of Jesus when he writes that He loves the church at Laodicea and thus, will hold them accountable. *(John 3:19)* God created fathers who love their children so much they will discipline, be consistent, and hold their children accountable, all the while loving them unconditionally.

A happy home and a disciplined home are not mutually exclusive. In fact, without discipline, there can be no lasting harmony in the home. Thus, Godly fathers set standards and enforce those standards fairly and consistently.

The Bible calls for discipline and
a recognition of authority.
Children must learn this at home.

Billy Graham

My son, do not despise the Lord's
discipline and do not resent his rebuke,
because the Lord disciplines those he loves,
as a father the son he delights in.

Proverbs 3:11-12 NIV

The fear of the Lord is the beginning
of knowledge, but fools despise
wisdom and discipline.

Proverbs 1:7 NIV

He who heeds discipline shows the way to life,
but whoever ignores correction leads others astray.

Proverbs 10:17 NIV

...Folly is loud; she is undisciplined and
without knowledge.

Proverbs 9:13 NIV

The alternative to discipline is disaster.

Vance Havner

*W*ithhold not correction from the child....

Proverbs 23:13 KJV

Chapter 10

and God Created Fathers...
Who Love Their Wives

Husbands, love your wives, just as Christ
loved the church and gave himself up for her....
Ephesians 5:25

There are many gifts a father can give his child, but there are few gifts greater than the gift of loving the child's mother. Children are blessed when they can witness firsthand the mutual love and respect of a mature father and mother whose love affair is expressed through words and actions. When parents love each other in a deep, committed relationship, children know, and they are blessed by that knowledge.

God intends that husbands love, honor, and cherish their wives. Jesus used this loving relationship to describe his relationship with the church. In each case, love is sacrificial and committed to the point of giving one's own life for the other.

Countless books describe the sanctity of marriage. The ultimate Book has this to say, "Nevertheless, let each individual among you also love his own wife even as himself, and let the wife see to it that she respect her husband." (Ephesians 5:33 NASB) That's simple advice, yet as timely today as it was the day it was penned by Paul almost two thousand years ago.

A father's responsibilities are many, but they begin with love for his God and his family. Family love begins when a husband treasures his wife faithfully and unconditionally.

1 Corinthians 13

If I speak in the tongues of men and of angels, but have not love, I am only a resounding gong or a clanging cymbal. If I have the gift of prophecy and can fathom all mysteries and all knowledge, and if I have a faith that can move mountains, but have not love, I am nothing. If I give all I possess to the poor and surrender my body to the flames, but have not love, I gain nothing.

Love is patient, love is kind. It does not envy, it does not boast, it is not proud. It is not rude, it is not self-seeking, it is not easily angered, it keeps no record of wrongs. Love does not delight in evil but rejoices with the truth. It always protects, always trusts, always hopes, always perseveres.

Love never fails. But where there are prophecies, they will cease; where there are tongues, they will be stilled; where there is knowledge, it will pass away. For we know in part and we prophesy in part, but when perfection comes, the imperfect disappears. When I was a child, I talked like a child, I thought like a child, I reasoned like a child. When I became a man, I put childish ways behind me. Now we see but a poor reflection as in a mirror; then we shall see face to face. Now I know in part; then I shall know fully, even as I am fully known.

And now these three remain: faith, hope and love. But the greatest of these is love.

1 Corinthians 13:1-13 NIV

Charm is deceptive, and beauty is fleeting;
  but a woman who fears the Lord is to be praised.
    Give her the reward she has earned....

Proverbs 31:31 NIV

Who can find a virtuous woman?
        For her price is far above rubies.

Proverbs 31:10 KJV

A virtuous woman is a crown to her husband....

Proverbs 12:4 KJV

Husbands and wives who live happily
ever after learn early to give and take,
to reach agreement by mutual consent.
A man with an unmoveable backbone is in
real trouble. God made backbones that can
stand rigid but can also bend when necessary.

Vance Havner

Let love and faithfulness never leave you
...write them on the tablet of your heart.

Proverbs 3:3 NIV

Chapter 11

and God Created Fathers...
Who Teach Truth

And the things you have heard me say in the presence
of many witnesses entrust to reliable men who will also
be qualified to teach others.

2 Timothy 2:2

Mr. James Medlin is a father, grandfather, and great-grandfather. He is a man of integrity who has touched the lives of his children in countless ways. To know Mr. Medlin is to love him: If ever there were a "straight shooter," he fits that description. He works hard, tells the truth, and expects others to do likewise. In short, James Medlin is a God-fearing, salt-of-the-earth, tell-it-like-it-is American, and darned proud of it, thank you very much.

"Pa" Medlin (as he is known to us) has a straightforward philosophy of dealing with others. He says, "Treat everybody with honesty and respect, and deal generously with the other fellow. If you always give a little more than you have to, you'll always come out ahead in the end." This philosophy, of course, works.

We live in a world that glorifies the quick fix and the easy profit. Sometimes, the values espoused by men like James Medlin seem outdated and old-fashioned—thank goodness they are not. The principles of hard work and honest dealing are as valid today as they were in the Garden of Eden, and needed just as badly now as then.

Paul writes, "Concentrate on doing your best for God, work you won't be ashamed of, laying out the truth plain and simple. Stay clear of pious talk that is only talk. Words are not mere words, you know. If they're not backed by a godly life, they accumulate as poison in the soul." *(2 Timothy 2:15 The Message)* In other words, we are commanded to tell the truth and to live it.

Jesus says that the truth will set us free. *(John 8:32)* It follows that when we live lives of dishonesty and deceit, we sentence ourselves to prison cells of our own construction. God created fathers to tell the truth, to live the truth, and to teach the truth.

The Lord tested Abraham when He asked Abraham to sacrifice his son Isaac. Abraham was obedient, the Lord spared Isaac, and the Lord sent an angel with the message, "I swear by myself, declares the LORD, that because you have done this and have not withheld your son, your only son, I will surely bless you and make your descendants as numerous as the stars in the sky and as the sand on the seashore. Your descendants will take possession of the cities of their enemies, and through your offspring all nations on earth will be blessed, because you have obeyed me." *(Genesis 22:15-18)* God blessed Abraham, and He is still in the business of blessing obedient fathers *and* their children.

God-fearing fathers ask themselves this question: "Will I leave my children and grandchildren a legacy of honesty and fair-dealing, or will I be for them an example of expediency and short-cuts?" The better legacy is self-evident; honesty remains the best policy, just as honest men remain the best role models. Righteous fathers serve as lasting examples to their families because righteous fathers measure up to God's standards.

The man of integrity walks securely,
but he who takes crooked paths
will be found out.

Proverbs 10 9 NIV

Integrity is not a given factor in everyone's life.
It is a result of self-discipline, inner trust,
and a decision to be relentlessly honest
in all situations in our lives.

John Maxwell

A little lie is like a little pregnancy — it doesn't
take long before everyone knows.

C. S. Lewis

Long ago I ceased to count heads.
Truth is often in the minority in this evil world.

C. H. Spurgeon

Buy the truth and do not sell it;
get wisdom, discipline,
and understanding.

Proverbs 23:23 NIV

And ye shall know the truth,
and the truth shall make you free.

John 8:32 KJV

Therefore laying aside falsehood, speak truth
each one of you with his neighbor,
for we are members of one another.

Ephesians 4:25 NASB

... add to your faith virtue; and to virtue, knowledge....

II Peter 1:5 KJV

and God Created Fathers...
Who Are Forever

———◆———

Love never fails. But where there are prophecies,
they will cease; where there are tongues,
they will be stilled; where there is knowledge;
it will pass away.

1 Corinthians 13:8

The candle business has lit up the merchandizing landscape in recent years. This multi-million dollar business offers a myriad of shapes, sizes, and scents. My daughter introduced me to the art of relaxation with candles. Scented candles can provide a soothing effect after a hectic day by engaging the senses of sight and smell. But, there is a more important effect of candles on my life — the effect of remembrance. When I was growing up, every Christmas Eve, somewhere in the house there was a silver candleholder with a white candle burning. My dad lit this candle every year in memory of his mother.

Now, every Christmas Eve, I light a green candle in memory of my dad, green because of his Irish heritage. I take time to sip some Irish Crème coffee, watch the candlelight flicker on the wall, and remember. I remember his love, his care, his encouragement, the way he celebrated life, his dedication to his God, his servant heart, the truth he taught, his patience in nurturing me, the time he spent with me, his loving discipline, and his commitment and love to my mother. I recall events and experiences that make me laugh and make me cry. And, though my father has been gone from this world for many years, I treasure his presence through memory.

The apostle Paul asks, "Who shall separate us from the love of Christ?" He answers his question, "For I am convinced that neither death nor life, neither angels nor demons, neither the present nor the future, nor any powers, neither height nor depth, not anything else in all creation, will be able to separate us from the love of God that is in Christ Jesus our Lord." *(Romans 8:35,38,39)*

If your father is alive, tell him you love him today. If he has passed on, remember that nothing can separate you from your father's love, not even death. God blesses each of us with joyous memories that give us strength until we are reunited with our loved ones in heaven.

If you have the privilege of being called "Dad" by one or more loving sons or daughters, consider yourself among the luckiest men on earth. Then, get busy loving your family with the firm assurance that your love will be felt for generations to come. After all, when God created a father's love, he created enough to last a lifetime...and beyond.

Children's children are the crown
of old men; and the glory of children
are their fathers.

Proverbs 17:6 KJV

Scripture Verses
for Fathers

Godly Fathers Exercise Patience

And the servant of the Lord must not strive;
but be gentle unto all men, apt to teach, patient;
in meekness instructing those that
oppose themselves …

II Timothy 2:24-25 KJV

The Lord is wonderfully good to those who wait
for him and seek him. So it is good to wait
quietly for salvation from the Lord.

Lamentations 3: 25-26 NLT

Better a patient man than a warrior, a man who
controls his temper than one who takes a city.

Proverbs 16:32 NIV

Don't be impatient for the Lord to act!
Travel steadily along his path.
He will honor you….

Psalm 37:34 NLT

Godly Fathers Praise the Lord

Praise ye the LORD. O give thanks unto
the LORD; for he is good:
for his mercy endureth forever.

Psalm 106:1 KJV

I will praise thee, O LORD, with my whole heart;
I will show forth all thy marvelous works.
I will be glad and rejoice in thee:
I will sing praise to thy name, O thou Most High.

Psalm 9:1-2 KJV

Let my mouth be filled with thy praise and
with thy honor all the day.

Psalm 71:8 KJV

I will praise thee with my whole heart....

Psalm 138:1 KJV

Godly Fathers are Praying Fathers

And whatsoever we ask, we receive of him,
because we keep his commandments, and
do those things that are pleasing in his sight.

1 John 3:15 KJV

Rejoice evermore. Pray without ceasing.
In every thing give thanks: for this
is the will of God in Christ Jesus concerning you.

1 Thessalonians 5:16-18 KJV

The effective prayer of a righteous man
can accomplish much.

James 5:16 NASB

And he withdrew himself into the wilderness,
and prayed.

Luke 5:16 KJV

Godly Fathers are Humble

...and all of you, clothe yourselves with humility
toward one another, for God is opposed to the proud,
but gives grace to the humble.

1 Peter 5:5 NASB

Blessed are the meek, for they will inherit the earth.

Matthew 5:5 NIV

And what does the Lord require of you?
    To act justly and to love mercy and
        to walk humbly with your God.

Micah 6:8 NIV

Before his downfall a man's heart is proud,
    but humility comes before honor.

Proverbs 18:12 NIV

Godly Fathers Live Righteously

Blessed are those who hunger and thirst for
    righteousness, for they will be filled.

Matthew 5:6 NIV

Teach me to do thy will; for thou art my God:
    thy Spirit is good; lead me into
        the land of uprightness.

Psalm 143:10 KJV

The LORD rewarded me according to
    my righteousness....

Psalm 18:20 KJV

The steps of a good man are ordered
    by the LORD....

Psalm 37:23 KJV

Godly Fathers Share the Gospel

For by grace are ye saved through faith;
    and that not of yourselves: it is the gift of God:
      not of works, lest any man should boast.

Ephesians 2:8-9 KJV

For God so loved the world, that he gave his only
    begotten Son, that whosoever believeth in him
      should not perish, but have everlasting life.

John 3:16 KJV

These things have I written unto you that believe
    on the name of the Son of God;
      that ye may know that ye have eternal life....

1 John 5:13 KJV

It is a trustworthy statement, deserving full
    acceptance, that Christ Jesus came into
      the world to save sinners....

1 Timothy 1:15 NASB

Godly Fathers Resist Temptation

There hath no temptation taken you but such as
is common to man: but God is faithful,
who will not suffer you to be tempted above that ye
are able; but will with the temptation also make a
way to escape, that ye may be able to bear it.

I Corinthians 10:13 KJV

... be vigilant; because your adversary the devil,
as a roaring lion, walketh about,
seeking whom he may devour.

I Peter 5:8 KJV

... the Lord knoweth how to deliver the godly
out of temptation ....

II Peter 2:9 KJV

Blessed is the man that endureth temptation:
for when he is tried,
he shall receive the crown of life....

James 1:12 KJV

Godly Fathers Give Thanks

And let the peace of God rule in your hearts…
and be ye thankful.

Colossians 3:15 KJV

In everything give thanks; for this is God's will
for you in Christ Jesus.

1 Thessalonians 5:18 NIV

Finally, brethren, whatsoever things are true,
whatsoever things are honest,
whatsoever things are just,
whatsoever things are pure,
whatsoever things are lovely,
whatsoever things are of good report;
if there be any virtue,
and if there be any praise,
think on these things.

Philippians 4:8 KJV

Godly Fathers Trust in God

It is better to trust in the LORD than
to put confidence in man. It is better to trust
in the LORD than to put confidence in princes.

Psalm 118:8-9 KJV

The LORD is my rock, and my fortress,
and my deliverer; my God, my strength,
in whom I will trust....

Psalm 18:2 KJV

In God have I put my trust:
I will not be afraid what man can do unto me.

Psalm 56:11 KJV

Trust ye in the LORD forever: for in
the LORD JEHOVAH is everlasting strength.

Isaiah 26:4 KJV

Godly Fathers Love Truth

And ye shall know the truth,
　　and the truth shall make you free.

John 8:32 KJV

Therefore laying aside falsehood,
　　speak truth each one of you with his neighbor,
　　for we are members of one another.

Ephesians 4:25 NASB

… as we have received mercy, we faint not;
　　but have renounced the hidden things of
dishonesty, not walking in craftiness, nor handling
the word of God deceitfully; but, by manifestation
　　of the truth, commending ourselves to
　　every man's conscience in the sight of God.

II Corinthians 4:1-2 KJV

To this end was I born, and for this cause came I into
the world, that I should bear witness unto the truth.

John 18:37 KJV

Godly Fathers Seek Wisdom

Let the word of Christ dwell in you richly
in all wisdom; teaching and admonishing
one another in psalms and hymns and
spiritual songs, singing with grace
in your hearts to the Lord.

Colossians 3:16 KJV

If any of you lack wisdom, let him ask of God,
that giveth to all men liberally,
and upbraideth not;
and it shall be given him.

James 1:5 KJV

...the wisdom that is from above is first pure,
then peaceable, gentle, and easy to be entreated,
full of mercy and good fruits, without partiality,
and without hypocrisy.

James 3:17 KJV

Godly Fathers Resist Worry

Let not your heart be troubled:
>ye believe in God, believe also in me.

>*John 14:1 KJV*

Come to me all you who are weary and burdened,
and I will give you rest. Take my yoke upon you
and learn from me, for I am gentle and humble
in heart, and you will find rest for your soul.
For my yoke is easy and my burden is light.

>*Matthew 11:28-30 NIV*

An anxious heart weighs a man down....

>*Proverbs 12:25 NIV*

Peace I leave with you, my peace I give unto you:
>not as the world giveth, give I unto you.
Let not your heart be troubled,
neither let it be afraid.

>*John 14:27 KJV*

Godly Fathers Love Their Children

Train a child in the way he should go,
and when he is old he will not turn from it.

Proverbs 22:6 NIV

Children's children are the crown of old men;
and the glory of children are their fathers.

Proverbs 17:6 KJV

And Jesus called a little child unto him,
and set him in the midst of them, and said,
Verily I say unto you, Except ye be converted,
and become as little children, ye shall not enter into
the kingdom of heaven.

Matthew 18:2-3 KJV

And whoever welcomes a little child like this
in my name welcomes me.

Matthew 18:5 NIV

Godly Fathers Are Courageous

The Lord himself goes before you and
will be with you; he will never leave you
nor forsake you. Do not be afraid;
do not be discouraged.

Deuteronomy 31:8 NIV

Be strong and courageous, and do the work.
Do not be afraid or discouraged, for the Lord God,
my God, is with you.

1 Chronicles 28:20 NIV

For God hath not given us the spirit of fear;
but of power, and of love, and of a sound mind.

II Timothy 1:7 KJV

I can do everything through him
that gives me strength.

Philippians 4:13 NIV

About the Author

Jim Gallery lives and writes in Middle Tennessee. He serves as senior editor for both Brighton Books and Walnut Grove Press. In addition, Jim is a sought-after speaker and lecturer who has 20 years of experience as a pastor.

Jim is a graduate of the University of South Florida and the New Orleans Baptist Theological Seminary. He is the father of two children.

Some of his other titles include:

God Can Handle It
God Can Handle It... Teenagers
Prayers of a Godly Woman
Prayers of a Dedicated Teacher
Prayers of a Righteous Man
And God Created... Mothers
And God Created... Angels